KANJI
de MANGA
Vol. 5

MANGA UNIVERSITY presents...

Kanji de Manga

漢字 で マンガ

The Comic Book That Teaches You How To Read And Write Japanese!

volume 5

Created by Glenn Kardy   Art by Chihiro Hattori

Japanime

TOKYO   SAN FRANCISCO

Manga University Presents ... Kanji de Manga
The Comic Book That Teaches You
How To Read And Write Japanese
Volume Five

Published by Manga University under the auspices of Japanime Co. Ltd.,
3-31-18 Nishi-Kawaguchi, Kawaguchi-shi, Saitama-ken 332–0021, Japan.

www.mangauniversity.com

First edition,

ISBN-13: 978-4-921205-10-2
ISBN-10: 4-921205-10-8

07 08 09 10   10 9 8 7 6 5 4 3 2 1

Printed in Canada

CONTENTS

The Manga University
Mission Statement

The mission of Manga University is to enlighten and educate the international community on all aspects of Japanese culture through the creative use of traditional manga artwork.

The university recognizes that manga transcends mainstream entertainment and possesses a unique ability to convey the true spirit of Japan, making the art form an ideal communicative tool to touch the lives and inspire the minds of Japan enthusiasts worldwide.

Our mission and philosophy are firmly rooted in the principles and conviction of the Japanese educational tradition and in the best ideals of Japanese heritage.

Founded at the turn of the century and located in Tokyo, Manga University is one of the world's foremost publishers of manga-themed educational materials.

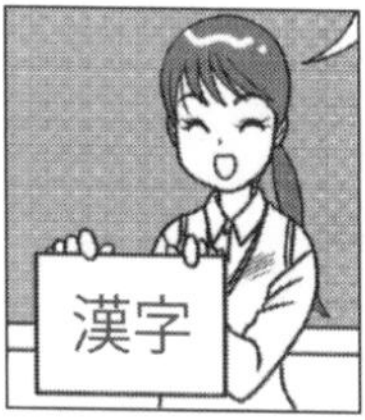
漢字

INTRODUCTION

Welcome to another semester at Manga University! It may seem like only yesterday that you began your journey into learning how to read and write Japanese kanji. If so, great — because that means you've been having fun the whole time. And with four volumes of Kanji de Manga under your belt, you can stride with confidence into the next level of advanced characters.

However, it's important to remember that kanji is not an alphabet, and memorizing thousands of characters is not as easy as ABC — not even for the Japanese themselves!

In fact, studying kanji is like learning to play a sport. Once you've got the fundamentals down, you explore new techniques but continue to practice the basics to stay in shape. So while you're working your way through this book, take some time to look back at earlier volumes of *Kanji de Manga* to see how many characters you remember.

Due to the pen being rapidly replaced by the computer and cellphone, even people in Japan have to go out of their way to practice writing kanji to stay fresh. Many Japanese now carry electronic dictionaries to look up old or complex characters. There are several kanji-learning video games, and television game shows often have kanji questions, the most difficult of which very few contestants can answer.

What does this mean for you?

It means that it doesn't take a consummate mastery of kanji to read and write everyday Japanese. It also means that with the dedication that you've already shown by making your way through the first four volumes of *Kanji de Manga,* nothing can stop you from obtaining the same level of kanji expertise as a native Japanese reader.

Upon completing this volume, you will have learned a total of four-hundred Japanese characters. That should be enough to get you through your favorite manga text or young-adult novel — and maybe even win you a little prize money! Just don't be intimidated by how much more kanji there is out there, because a dedicated student never really stops learning. And as long as you're learning kanji, we'd like you to learn it from us.

So, let's begin with two new kanji: 頑張つて！(Ganbatte!)

PAGE GUIDE

② HOT
③ あつ(い)、ショ
① 暑
ex. 暑い (あつい) - hot
④ ex. 残暑* (ざんしょ) - Indian summer
ex. 猛暑* (もうしょ) - heat wave
⑤
⑥
きせつはあきなのに
まだまだ
暑いね〜…。
ざん暑がすごいね。
なかなかすずしく
ならないもんだね。
⑦ First boy: きせつはあきなのに
まだまだ暑いね〜・・・。
Even though it's already fall,
it's still really hot outside.
Second boy: ざん暑がすごいね。
なかなかすずしくならないもんだね。
Indian summer is crazy like that.
It just doesn't get cool.

① The featured kanji
② Common definition
③ Readings: kun-yomi (Japanese readings) are written in hiragana, while on-yomi (Chinese readings) are in katakana.
④ Examples of compounds containing the featured kanji, their pronunciations (written in hiragana) and English definitions. (An asterisk next to a compound indicates that one or more of its kanji are not featured in this or any of the previous volumes of the *Kanji de Manga* series.)
⑤ Stroke order: In general, the strokes are written from top to bottom and left to right. For a list of additional stroke-order rules, please refer to the chart at the back of this book.
⑥ The manga. All dialogue is written in hiragana and katakana except for the single featured kanji. The proper pronunciation of the kanji is indicated in furigana (tiny hiragana) written above the character.
⑦ Translation of the dialogue and selected onomatopoeia.

Kanji de Manga

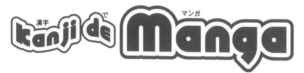

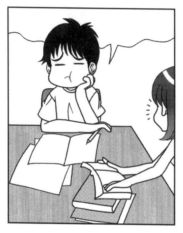

STUDY SECTION

TOGETHER

あい、ショウ、ソウ

ex. 相性* (あいしょう) - compatibility
ex. 相手 (あいて) - partner
ex. 相談 (そうだん) - consultation

一	十	才	木	杧	机	相
相	相					

手相

手相占い

占

そう
て相うらないだ。
れんあいについて
うらなってもらっちゃお！

ことしは
あい
すてきな相てが
そう
みつかるて相が
でているわよ。

きゃー！
やったー！

がんばるぞー！！

Girl: て相うらないだ。れんあいに
ついてうらなってもらっちゃお！
Oh, a palm reader. I'll have her
check my hand for love-lines!

Sign: 手相占い (palm reader)

Sign: 占 (fortune-teller)

Palm reader: ことしはすてきな相て
がみつかるて相がでているわよ。
It seems to me that this year you're
going to find a dreamy partner.

Girl: きゃー！やったー！がんばるぞー！！
Ye-esss! All right! I'm going for broke!!

SELLING

あきな(う)、ショウ

ex. 商品* (しょうひん) - product
ex. 商標* (しょうひょう) - trademark
ex. 商売 (しょうばい) - trade business

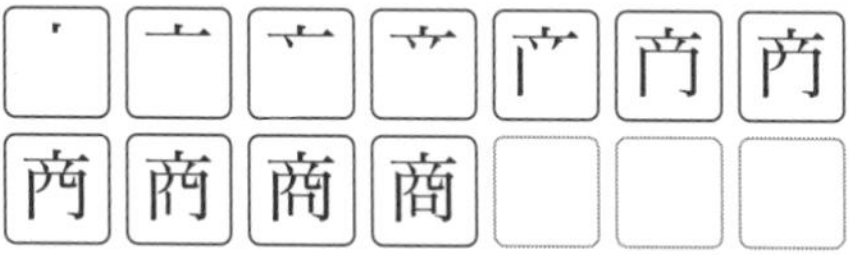

しょう
商ばいするのって
やっぱり
たいへん？

そりゃぁ、
しょう
商ばいは
らくじゃないさ。

しょう
商ひんかんりから
いろいろなしごとが
あるし。

なにより
おくさんがこわい…。

何
油
を
売
っ
て
い
る
の
？

コソ…

Boy: 商ばいするのってやっぱり
たいへん？ So sales is pretty tough?
Store owner: そりゃぁ、商ばいはらく
じゃないさ。Well, sales is no picnic.
商ひんかんりからいろいろな
しごとがあるし。There are a lot of
aspects to managing a store.

Store owner: なによりおくさんがこわい…。
Above all, my wife terrifies me...

コソ・・・ (furtively)

Wife: 何油を売っているの？
What are you doing loafing about!?

温

WARM

あたた(かい)、オン

ex. 温泉* (おんせん) - hot springs
ex. 気温 (きおん) - outside temperature
ex. 体温 (たいおん) - body temperature

きょうはき温（おん）がひくくてさむいね。
こんなひは温（おん）せんにでもつかって温（あたた）まりたいね。

First girl: きょうはき温がひくくてさむいね。
The temperature dropped today and now it's cold.

Second girl: こんなひは温せんにでもつかって温まりたいね。
On a day like this I just want to go to the hot springs and warm up.

HOT

あつ(い)、ショ

ex. 暑い (あつい) - hot
ex. 残暑* (ざんしょ) - Indian summer
ex. 猛暑* (もうしょ) - heat wave

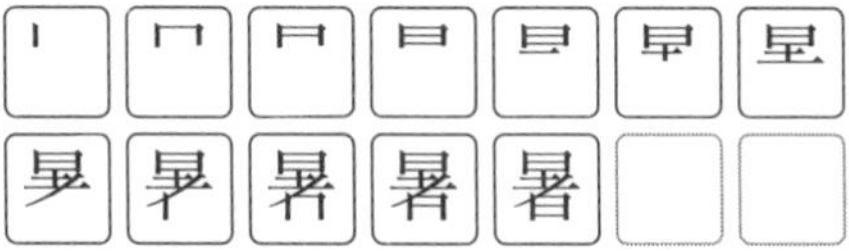

一	丌	日	戸	旦	早	星
星	昇	界	暑	暑		

きせつはあきなのに
まだまだ
暑いね～…。

ざん暑がすごいね。
なかなかすずしく
ならないもんだね。

First boy: きせつはあきなのに
まだまだ暑いね～・・・。
Even though it's already fall,
it's still really hot outside.

Second boy: ざん暑がすごいね。
なかなかすずしくならないもんだね。
Indian summer is crazy like that.
It just doesn't get cool.

DIAGRAM

あらわ(す)、おもて、ヒョウ

ex. 表す (あらわす) - to express
ex. 表 (おもて) - surface
ex. 表情* (ひょうじょう) - facial expression

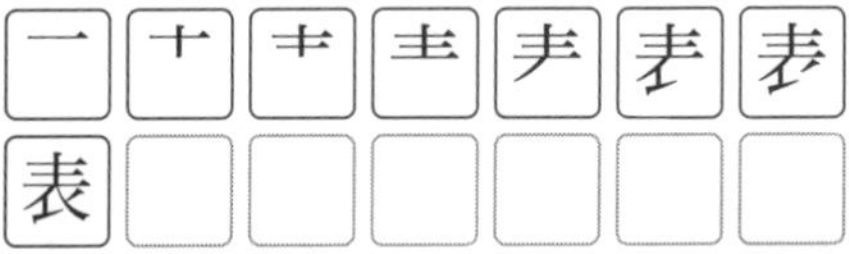

| 一 | 十 | 圭 | 圭 | 丰 | 丰 | 丢 |
| 表 | | | | | | |

はーい、
プリントを表(おもて)にかえして
みてー。

ぺら ぺらっ ぺら

そこに表(ひょう)が
のっていると
おもうけど、

その表(ひょう)がなにを
表(あらわ)しているか
かんがえて、

したに
かいて
みよう。

||はーーい||

Teacher: はーい、プリントを
表にかえしてみてー。
OK now, please turn
the handout over.

ぺらぺらっぺら (sheets of
paper being flipped over)

Teacher: そこに表がのっているとおもうけど、
There's a diagram on it...

その表がなにを表しているかかんがえて、
したにかいてみよう。Think about what the chart
expresses, then write your answers underneath.

Students (in unison): はーい Ye-esss!

PLANT

う(える)、う(わる)、ショク

ex. 植える (うえる) - to plant
ex. 植木 (うえき) - potted plant
ex. 植物 (しょくぶつ) - plant life; flora

ここのスペース
なにもなくて
さびしいわね。

うーん…
そうだなぁ。

植（しょく）ぶつでも植（う）えて、
かだんにしてみるというのは
どうかな？

わぁ、すてきな
アイデアね。

Girl: ここのスペースなにもなくてさびしいわね。
This space feels so empty without anything in it.

Boy: うーん・・・そうだなぁ。
Yeah... you're right.

Boy: 植ぶつでも植えて、かだんにしてみるというのはどうかな？
What do you think about planting some plants and making a flower bed here?

Girl: わぁ、すてきなアイデアね。
Oh, that's a wonderful idea.

受

RECEIVE

う(かる)、う(ける)、ジュ

ex. 受付* (うけつけ) - reception
ex. 受ける (うける) - to receive
ex. 受章 (じゅしょう) - receive a medal

受(う)かったぁぁぁぁぁ!!!
しぼう だいがくに ごうかく したぞ!

これでやっと、あのつらい 受(じゅ)けんじごくから かいほうされる…。
あと 10日

Boy: 受かったぁぁぁぁぁ!!!
I paaaaaased!!!
しぼうだいがくにごうかくしたぞ!
I got into my first-choice college!

これでやっと、あのつらい受けんじごくからかいほうされる・・・。
I've finally been liberated from the agony of college entrance exams.

Sign: あと10日
Ten more days (until the exam)

STRIKE

う(ち)、う(つ)、ダ

ex. 打つ (うつ) - to hit
ex. 強打 (きょうだ) - a heavy blow
ex. 打者 (だしゃ) - baseball batter

つくえのかどで
あしを打った
みたいよ。

またぁ?

あ…つぎはたなで
あたまをきょう打。

みていて
あきないひとだね。

ガツン (klunk)

Boy: いてー!
Ouch!

First girl: つくえのかどであしを打ったみたいよ。
It looks like he hit his foot on the edge of that desk.

Second girl: またぁ? Again?

First girl: あ・・・つぎはたなであたまをきょう打。
Oh, now he's gonna bang his head on the cabinet.

Second girl: みていてあきないわね。 He's fun to watch,
isn't he? ガッ (head banging) フラフラ (shuffling in pain)

BEAUTY

うつく(しい)、ビ、ミ

ex. 美しい (うつくしい) - beautiful
ex. 美人 (びじん) - beautiful person
ex. 美容院* (びよういん) - beauty salon

丶	丷	丷	丷	羊	羊	羊
羊	美					

うつく
美しい！

ホホホホ

やっぱり
わたしって
び
美じん！

ホーホホホ

すばらしい
みごとな
うつく
美しさだ!!

ヒクッ

すばらしい
いぬですね。

い…
いぬのこと
だった
の!?

Boy (unseen): 美しい！
Beautiful!

ホホホホ (haughty laughing)

Woman: やっぱりわたしって
美じん！ I must really be
a beautiful woman!

ホーホホホ (more
laughter)

Boy (unseen): すば
らしいみごとな美
しさだ!! What
amazingly superb
beauty!!

Boy: すばらしいいぬですね。
It really is a spectacular pup.

ヒクッ (embarrassed)

Woman: い・・・いぬの
ことだったの!? He...he's
talking about a dog!?

CENTER

央

オウ

ex. 中央 (ちゅうおう) - center
ex. 中央アジア (ちゅうおうアジア) - Central Asia
ex. 中央広場 (ちゅおうひろば) - central square

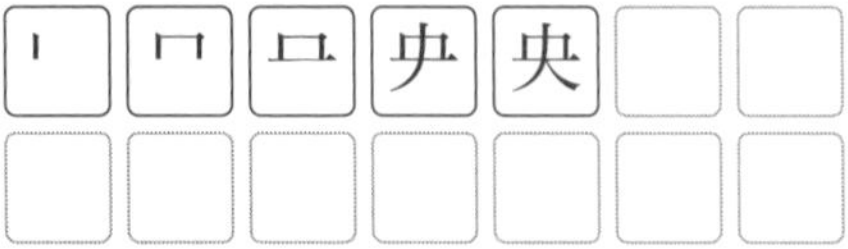

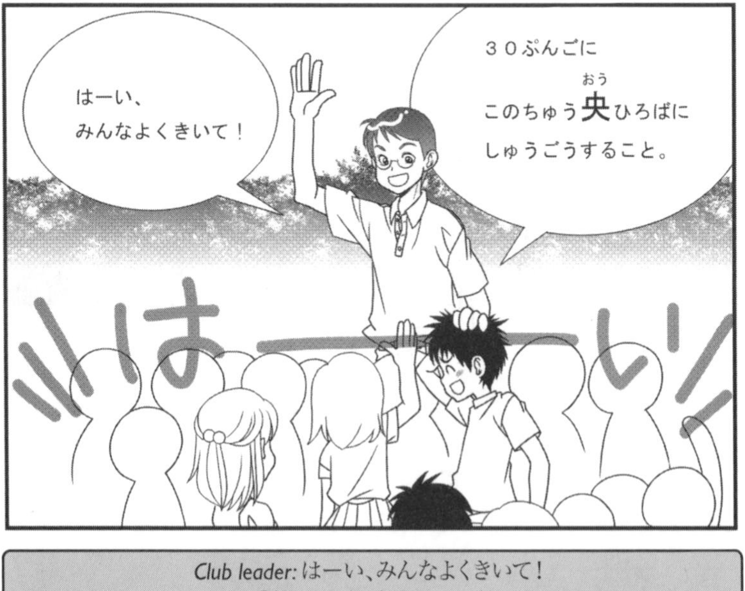
はーい、
みんなよくきいて！
３０ぷんごに
このちゅう央(おう)ひろばに
しゅうごうすること。
はーい

Club leader: はーい、みんなよくきいて！
OK, everybody listen up!
３０ぷんごにこのちゅう央ひろばにしゅうごうすること。
In 30 minutes, everyone meet back here in the center of this square.

Club members (in unison): はーい (Ye-esss!)

SWIM

およ(ぐ)、エイ

ex. 泳ぐ (およぐ) - to swim
ex. 競泳* (きょうえい) - swimming match
ex. 水泳 (すいえい) - a swim

`	⸍	氵	氵	汀	泙	泙
泳						

およ
泳ぐのだいすきだから
あしたからのすい泳の
じゅぎょうが
とっても
たのしみ！

およ
ぼくは泳ぐのとくいじゃないから
そうでもないけど…。

Girl: 泳ぐのだいすきだからあした
からのすい泳のじゅぎょうが
とってもたのしみ！
I love swimming, so I'm really
looking forward to the swim
class that begins tomorrow!

Boy: ぼくは泳ぐのとくいじゃない
からそうでもないけど・・・。
I'm not really good at
swimming, so I'm not quite as
excited...

STORY (LEVEL)

カイ

ex. 階級 (かいきゅう) - grade in school
ex. 階層* (かいそう) - social class
ex. 階段* (かいだん) - stairs

階

はぁ…
はぁ…
かい
ずっと階だんを
のぼるのもたいへんだなぁ…。
かい
なん階くらいまで
のぼったかなぁ…。

はぁ・・・はぁ・・・ (heavy breathing)

Boy: ずっと階だんをのぼるのもたいへんだなぁ・・・。
Climbing up all these stairs sure has been tough...
なん階くらいまでのぼったかなぁ・・・。
I wonder how many stories it's been...

PERSON IN CHARGE

かかり、かか(る)、ケイ

ex. 係 (かかり) - a duty
ex. 係員* (かかりいん) - an official
ex. 関係* (かんけい) - relationship

ノ	イ	イ	仔	伅	係	係
係	係					

しょうくん、いそがしいから
係がちがうけど
これはこぶの
てつだって。

ぼく、かん**係**ない**係**なのに〜。

まー、
まー。

Girl: しょうくん、いそがしいから係が
ちがうけどこれはこぶの
てつだって。
Hey, Shou-kun*. I know you're not
in charge of this department, but
could you help carry these?

Boy: ぼく、かん係ない係なのに〜。
But my position has nothing to do
with this.

Girl: まー、まー。
Oh, well.

*Shou (しょう) is the boy's name, and kun (くん) is an honorific.

GUEST / CLIENT

カク、キャク

ex. お客さん (おきゃくさん) - customer
ex. 客室 (きゃくしつ) - guest room
ex. 客観的* (きゃっかんてき) - objectively

`	``	宀	宀	宓	安	客
客	客					

きゃく
お**客**さんこなくてひまだね。

ふあああ…

うん…。

Clerk on left: お客さんこなくてひまだね。
Man, no customers are coming in and there's nothing to do.

ふあああ・・・ yawning

Clerk on right: うん・・・。
Yep...

VICTORY

か(つ)、まさ(る)、ショウ

ex. 勝つ (かつ) - to win
ex. 勝利* (しょうり) - success
ex. 優勝* (ゆうしょう) - victory

ノ 刀 月 月 月 月′ 月⺊

月⺊ 月⺊ 朕 勝 勝 ☐ ☐

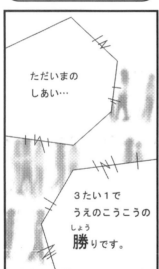

ただいまの
しあい…

３たい１で
うえのこうこうの
_{しょう}
勝りです。

_か
勝ったぁぁぁぁぁ !!!

_{しょう}
ゆう勝だー！

Announcer: ただいまのしあい・・・
And this match...

３たい１でうえのこうこうの勝りです。
...goes to Ueno High School, with a
final score of 3-1.

Crowd: 勝ったぁぁぁぁぁ!!!
We won!!!

Boy: ゆう勝だー！
Victory is ours!

SAD

かな(しい)、かな(しむ)、ヒ

ex. 悲しい (かなしい) - sad
ex. 慈悲* (じひ) - mercy
ex. 悲観* (ひかん) - pessimism

| ノ | ㇇ | ㇆ | ㇆ | �킈 | 非 | 非 |
| 非 | 非 | 悲 | 悲 | 悲 | | |

しけんにおちていたら
どうしよう…。

そんなに 悲かん
することないわよ。

でもぉ…。

そんなに 悲しまないでー！わたしまで
悲しくて　　なけてきちゃうわー！

First girl: しけんにおちていたら
どうしよう・・・。
I don't know what I'll do if I fail
the test...

Second girl: そんなに悲かんする
ことないわよ。
Don't be so pessimistic about it.

First girl: でもぉ・・・。　But...
じわ・・・ (tears running)

Second girl: そんなに悲しまないでー！わたし
までかなしくてなけてきちゃうわー！Don't be
so sad! Now you're making me want to cry!
しくしくしく (weeping)　わーん (waah)

GOD / SOUL

かみ、かん、こう、シン、ジン

ex. 神様* (かみさま) - a god
ex. 神経* (しんけい) - nerves
ex. 神社 (じんじゃ) - Shinto shrine

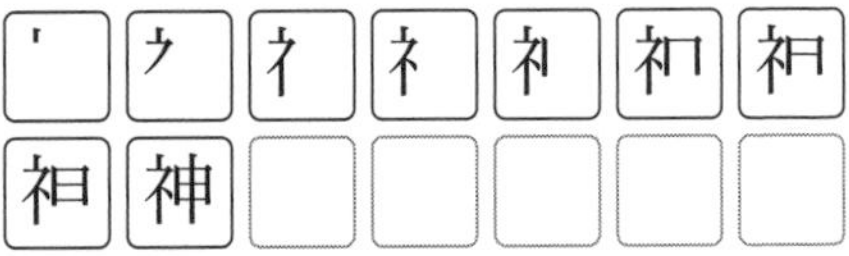

神

` ク ネ ネ ネ 祀 神
神 神

にほんの 神さまって
なんにんくらい
いるのかなぁ。

やおよろずの 神
なんていうくらい
だからね！

にょきっ

わぁっ！

あいかわらず
きみは 神しゅつきぼつ
だなぁ。
おどろいたよ。

まー
まー。

First boy: にほんの 神さまってなんにんくらいいるのかなぁ。 I wonder how many Japanese gods there are.

Second boy: やおよろずの神なんていうくらいだからね！ Enough to merit the phrase "8 million gods"!

にょきっ (sudden appearance)

First boy: わぁっ！ Yikes!

First boy: あいかわらずきみは神しゅつきぼつだなぁ。おどろいたよ。 As usual, you appear out of nowhere and scare me.

Second boy: まーまー。 Oh, well.

LIGHTLY

かる(い)、かろ(やか)、ケイ

ex. 軽い (かるい) - lightweight
ex. 軽快* (けいかい) - nimble
ex. 軽視* (けいし) - contempt

一　厂　𠂤　𠂤　亘　車　車

軒　軒　軽　軽　軽

かる
軽はずみでいってしまったけど
このにもつおもーい！
けい
軽ししすぎた
みたい。

てつだうよ。

ありがとう。
かる
軽くなったわ。

Girlfriend: 軽はずみでいってしまった
けどこのにもつおもーい！軽し
しすぎたみたい。
I was quick to say I'd help move this,
but this box is heavy! It looks like I
underestimated its weight.

Boyfriend: てつだうよ。
I'll help you out.

Girlfriend: ありがとう。軽くなったわ。
Thank you, it's much lighter now.

SKIN

かわ、ヒ

ex. 皮 (かわ) - skin; hide
ex. 皮膚* (ひふ) - skin
ex. 皮肉 (ひにく) - irony

ひにやけて**皮**ふが
まっくろだし、
皮もぼろぼろに
むけてきちゃったよ。

こむぎいろにやけたわね。

Boy: ひにやけて皮ふがまっくろだし、
皮もぼろぼろにむけてきちゃったよ。
My skin got sunburned, then it
became dark and is starting to flake
and peel off.

Girl: こむぎいろにやけたわね。
You've been toasted to a
golden brown.

TERM

キ、ゴ

ex. 学期 (がっき) - semester
ex. 期間 (きかん) - period
ex. 定期* (ていき) - fixed term

| 一 | 十 | 卄 | 卄 | 甘 | 其 | 其 |
| 其 | 期 | 期 | 期 | 期 | | |

きょうからがっ**期**まつテストをおこなう。

じゅんび**期**かんはたっぷりあったはずだぞ。

てんすうのわるかったものは、ついしをするからなー。

Teacher: きょうからがっ期まつテストをおこなう。
Beginning today, you'll have your end-of-semester exams.

Students (in unison): ええー！！
Really?!

Teacher: じゅんび期かんはたっぷりあったはずだぞ。 You should have had more than enough time to prepare.
てんすうのわるかったものは、ついしをするからなー。 Those with low grades will have to take another exam.

Students: えー！？そんなー What!? No way!

EXTINGUISH

き(える)、け(す)、ショウ

ex. 消える (きえる) - to disappear
ex. 消去 (しょうきょ) - deletion
ex. 消灯* (しょうとう) - turning off a light

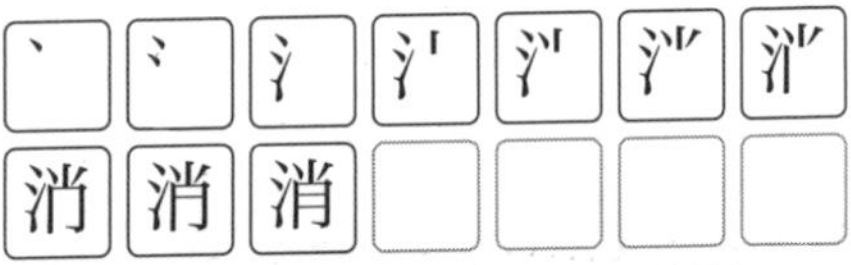

| ` | ` | ⺡ | ⺡ | ⺡ | ⺡ | ⺡ |
| 消 | 消 | 消 | | | | |

消とうの
じかんよー。

でんきを
消すわよ。

パッ

オバケやしきみたーい！
わーい

ドタドタ　バタ

でんきを消しても
うるさい…。

Mother: 消とうのじかんよー。でんきを消すわよ。All right kids, it's time for lights out. I'm turning them off now.

ドタバタ (slam-bang)

わーわー (yippee!)

パッ
(sudden darkness)

Children: オバケやしきみたーい！わーい Yay! It's like a haunted house!

Mother: でんきを消してもうるさい・・・。Even with the lights off they make a racket.

BEACH

きし、ガン

ex. 海岸 (かいがん) - beach
ex. 岸 (きし) - coast
ex. 岸辺* (きしべ) - riverbank

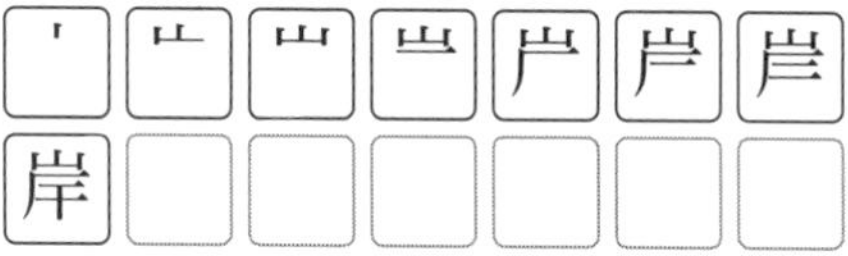

` 屵屵屵屵屵 岸`

がん
かい岸にだれかいるよ。
いってみよう。

ぎし
むこう岸から
およいできたんだ。

ええええ！？
すごいきょり
あるよ！

Girl: かい岸にだれかいるよ。いってみよう。
There's someone down on the beach. Let's check it out.

Boy: むこう岸からおよいできたんだ。
I just swam here from the opposite bank.
Girl: ええええ！？すごいきょりあるよ！
Really!? That's so far!

君

YOU (MALE)

きみ、ぎみ、クン

ex. 君 (きみ) - you

ex. 君が代 (きみがよ) - Japan's national anthem

ex. 諸君 (しょくん) - Ladies and Gentleman!

君！そこの君！
ノートをおとしたよ。
そこの君～!!
けんいち君、よばれているわよ。
はい、おとしもの。
ありごとうございます。

Teacher: 君！そこの君！ノートをおとしたよ。 You! You there! You dropped your notebook.

Teacher: そこの君～！！ You over there!!

Girl: けんいち君、よばれているわよ。 Kenichi-kun*, someone's calling you.

Teacher: はい、おとしもの。You dropped this.

Boy: ありがとうございます。Thank you.

*Kenichi (けんいち) is the boy's name, and kun (くん) is an honorific.

DECIDE

き(める)、き(まる)、ケツ

決

ex. 決める (きめる) - to decide
ex. 決定* (けってい) - decision
ex. 決心 (けっしん) - determination

くじびきで、だいひょうを
決めたいとおもいます。
くじ
ええー!!
決ていー!
トホホ…
おめでとう!

Teacher: くじびきで、だいひょうを決めたいとおもいます。
I'd like to decide the class leader by holding a random drawing.

くじ (lottery)

Students (in unison): ええー!! What?!

*Teacher:*決ていー!
It's been decided!

トホホ・・・ (humiliated boo-hooing)

当 (あたり; winner)

Students (in unison): おめでとう!
Congratulations!

級

RANK

キュウ

ex. 学級 (がっきゅう) - (school) class
ex. 級長 (きゅうちょう) - head of the class
ex. 高級 (こうきゅう) - high-grade

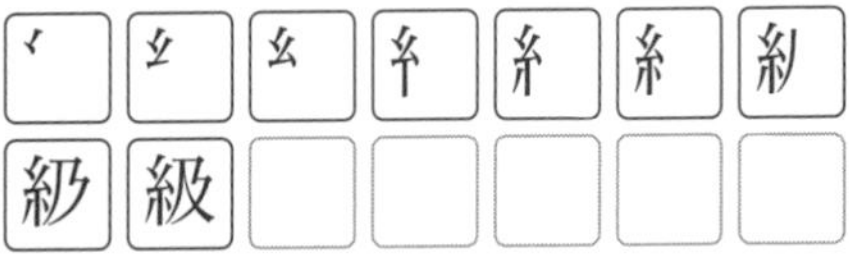

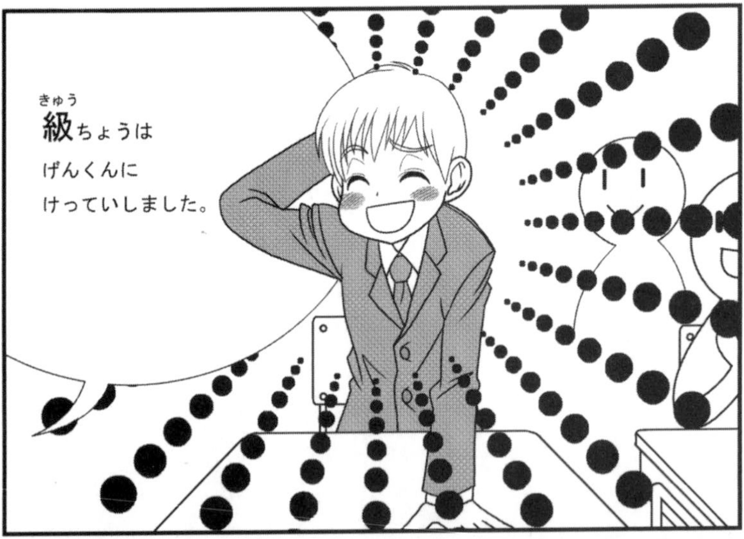
級(きゅう)ちょうは
げんくんに
けっていしました。

Teacher: 級ちょうはげんくんにけっていしました。
It's been decided that Gen-kun* is to be the head of the class.

*Gen (げん) is the student's name, and kun (くん) is an honorific.

BUREAU

キョク

ex. 局長 (きょくちょう) - office chief
ex. 結局* (けっきょく) - after all
ex. 郵便局* (ゆうびんきょく) - post office

゛	゛	尸	月	月	局	局

いま、ゆうびん**局**に
ゆうめいじんが
きているらしいよ。

みにいって
みようよ。

いちにち**局**ちょうを
しているみたいだね。

First boy: いま、ゆうびん局に
ゆうめいじんがきているらしいよ。
I just heard there's a famous
person coming to the post office.

Second boy: みにいってみようよ。
Let's check it out.

First boy: いちにち局ちょうをしている
みたいだね。
It looks like she's postmaster
for the day.

区

DISTRICT

ク

ex. 区 (く) - district
ex. 区域* (くいき) - territory
ex. 区役所* (くやくしょ) - district city hall

一 フ ㄨ 区

ここで区がわかれているみたいだよ。
世田谷区
このラインがめじるしで区べつしているみたいね。

First girl: ここで区がわかれているみたいだよ。
It looks like this is where the districts are separated.

Second girl: このラインがめじるしで区べつしているみたいね。
This line looks like the border that divides the two districts.

Sign in background: 世田谷区 (Setagaya-ku, a district of Tokyo)

WAREHOUSE

庫

ク、コ

ex. 在庫* (ざいこ) - inventory
ex. 倉庫* (そうこ) - warehouse
ex. 文庫本 (ぶんこぼん) - paperback book

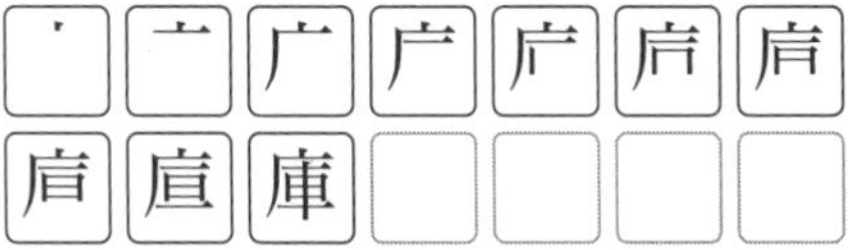

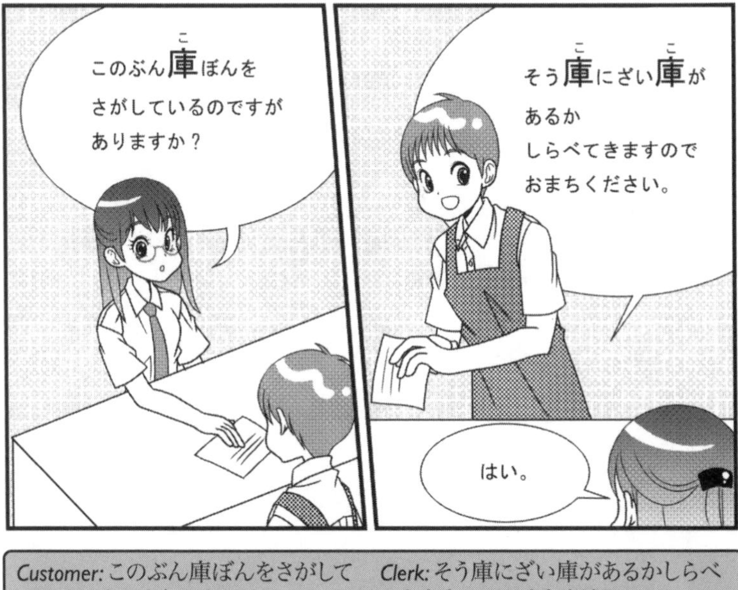
このぶん庫ぼんを さがしているのですが ありますか？
そう庫にざい庫が あるか しらべてきますので おまちください。
はい。

Customer: このぶん庫ぼんをさがしているのですがありますか？
I'm looking for this paperback. Do you have a copy?

Clerk: そう庫にざい庫があるかしらべてきますのでおまちください。
Our inventory is in the warehouse so I'll need to check there. Please wait a moment.

Customer: はい。OK.

UTENSIL

グ

ex. 家具 (かぐ) - furniture
ex. 具 (ぐ) - ingredients; means
ex. 道具 (どうぐ) - tools

| l | 冂 | 冃 | 月 | 目 | 且 | 具 |
| 具 | | | | | | |

具だくさんのカレーだね。

おいしそう！！

Boy: 具だくさんのカレーだね。おいしそう！！
This curry is loaded with different ingredients. It looks delicious!!

SUFFERING

くる(しい)、にが(い)、ク

ex. 苦しい (くるしい) - painful; difficult
ex. 苦労 (くろう) - hardship
ex. 苦い (にがい) - bitter

かぜで苦しそうね。
くすりのむ？

あのくすりは
苦いからいやだぁぁぁぁぁ！！！

わかった
わかった。

Sister: かぜで苦しそうね。
くすりのむ？
You look like you're really
suffering from that cold.
Why don't you take some medicine?

ぜーはーぜーはー・・・ (heavy breathing)

Brother: あのくすりは苦いから
いやだぁぁぁぁぁ！！！
I hate that medicine, it's so bitter!!!

Sister: わかったわかった。
OK, OK.

PREFECTURE

ケン

ex. 県 (けん) - prefecture
ex. 県庁* (けんちょう) - prefectural office
ex. 県民* (けんみん) - citizens of a prefecture

丨	冂	冃	目	目	䀠	皀
県	県					

にほんは４７の
とどうふ県にわかれているんだよ。

そうなんだ。

First student: にほんは４７のとどうふ県にわかれているんだよ。
Japan is broken up into 47 administrative divisions.
Second student: そうなんだ。
Oh, I see.

ICE

こおり、ひ、ヒョウ

ex. 氷 (こおり) - ice
ex. 氷河* (ひょうが) - glacier
ex. 氷点下 (ひょうてんか) - below freezing

氷

やけにさむいとおもったら…
ガチガチ
ブルッ
きおんが
ひょう
氷てんかだもんなぁ。
みずたまりに
こおり
氷がはってる！
パリン…
わーい。
こおり
氷わっちゃえ。

Boy: やけにさむいとおもったら・・・
It feels insanely cold out here...

きおんが氷てんかだもんなぁ。Probably because the temperature is below freezing.

ガチガチ (teeth chattering)

ブルッ (shivering)

みずたまりに氷がはってる！
Ice is forming in that puddle!

わーい。氷わっちゃえ。
All right! Time to break the ice.

パリン・・・ (ice cracking)

号

NUMBER

ゴウ

ex. 暗号* (あんごう) - code; password
ex. 号泣* (ごうきゅう) - crying aloud; wailing
ex. 信号* (しんごう) - stoplight

このゲーム、あん号をとくのがむずかしいなぁ。
ピコ ピコ ピコ
ここのあん号は、じゅんばんにならべればすぐとけるよ。
号きゅう…。
うわーんっ
ご…ごめんつい。
ときかたをおしえるなー！

First boy: このゲーム、あん号をとくのがむずかしいなぁ。 It's pretty difficult to crack the codes in this game.

ピコピコピコ (video game noises)

Second boy: ここのあん号は、じゅんばんにならべればすぐとけるよ。 All you have to do on this one is line the code up in sequential order.

First boy: ときかたをおしえるなー！ Don't tell me how to solve it! うわーんっ (crying)

Second boy: 号きゅう・・・。ご・・・ごめんつい。 He's really wailing... S... Sorry, dude.

HAPPINESS

さいわ(い)、しあわ(せ)、コウ

ex. 幸福*(こうふく) - happiness
ex. 幸せ (しあわせ) - good fortune
ex. 不幸 (ふこう) - bad luck

一	十	土	圡	幸	卋	幸
幸						

じかんをきにせず
ねていられるって
しあわ
幸せ〜！

こう
幸ふくなせいかつとは
まさにこのことかも…。

Brother: じかんをきにせず
ねていられるって幸せ〜！
I'm so happy to be able to sleep in
without worrying about the time!

ゴロゴロゴロ (rolling around in bed)

Sister: 幸ふくなせいかつとはまさに
このことかも・・・。
This must be the very definition of
happiness for him...

ごはんだよー。　おーい。
Hey! Breakfast is ready.

酒

ALCOHOL

さか、さけ、シュ

ex. お酒 (おさけ) - alcohol
ex. 酒屋 (さかや) - liquor store
ex. 日本酒 (にほんしゅ) - Japanese alcohol

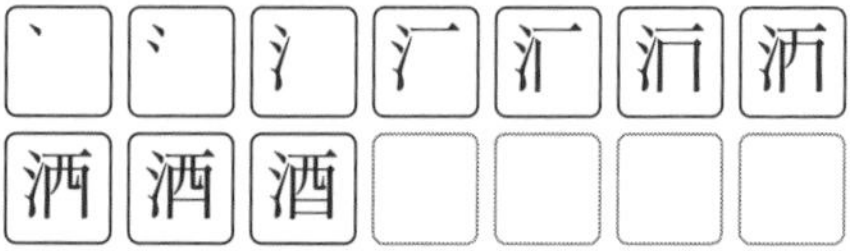

この酒やでビール、ワイン、にほん酒でも・・・。
お酒ってせかいじゅうにいろいろなしゅるいがたくさんあるんだなぁ。

Man: この酒やでビール、ワイン、にほん酒でも. . . 。
This liquor store has beer, wine, even Japanese sake...
お酒ってせかいじゅうにいろいろなしゅるいがたくさんあるんだなぁ。
There are certainly a lot of different kinds of liquor all over the world.

COLD

さむ(い)、カン

ex. 寒気 (かんき) - chill
ex. 寒い (さむい) - cold
ex. 防寒着* (ぼうかんぎ) - Windbreaker

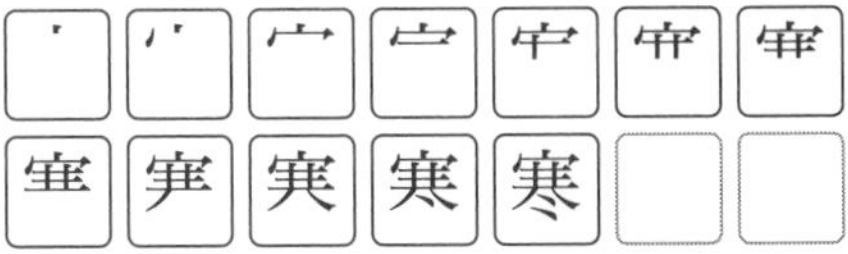

寒

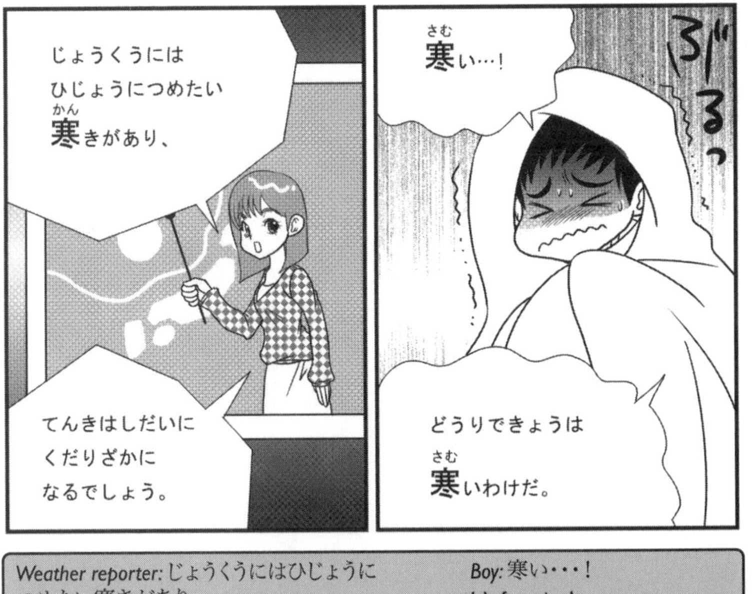

じょうくうには
ひじょうにつめたい
寒(かん)きがあり、
てんきはしだいに
くだりざかに
なるでしょう。
寒(さむ)い…!
ぶるっ
どうりできょうは
寒(さむ)いわけだ。

Weather reporter: じょうくうにはひじょうにつめたい寒きがあり、
What we see here is an extremely cold upper wind...
てんきはしだいにくだりざかになるでしょう。
...which will result in an immediate drop in temperatures.

Boy: 寒い・・・!
It's freezing!
ぶるっ (shivering)
どうりできょうは寒いわけだ
No wonder it's so cold today.

皿

DISH / PLATE

さら

ex. 小皿 (こざら) - saucer

ex. 皿 (さら) - plate

ex. 灰皿* (はいざら) - ashtray

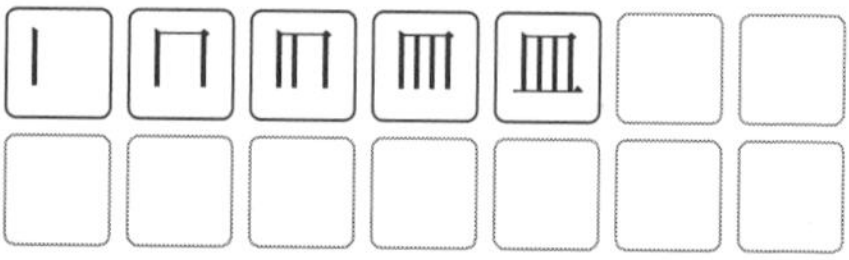

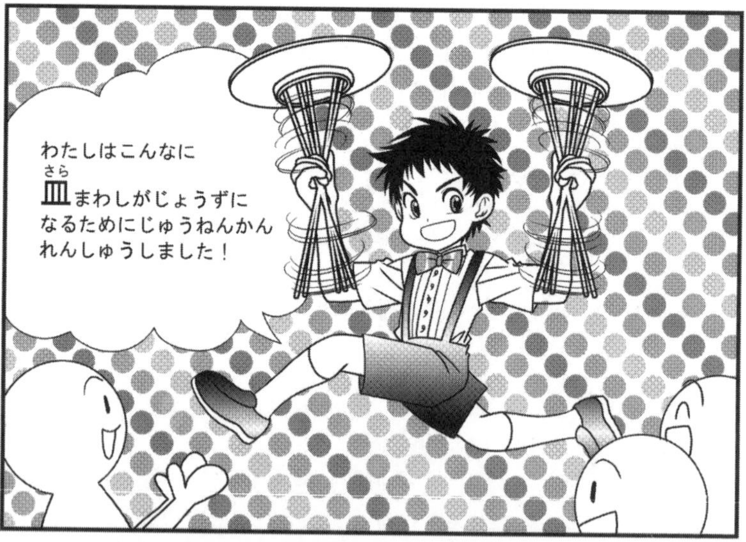
わたしはこんなに皿(さら)まわしがじょうずになるためにじゅうねんかんれんしゅうしました！

Circus performer: わたしはこんなに皿まわしがじょうずになるためにじゅうねんかんれんしゅうしました！

I practiced for 10 years before I got this good at plate-spinning!

POETRY

シ

ex. 詩 (し) - poem
ex. 詩集 (ししゅう) - book of poetry
ex. 詩人 (しじん) - poet

まるでおどるように
はなびらが
ちってゆくわ…。

詩じんだなぁ…。

はかなさの
なかにも
きらめく
そのかがやき…。

Girl: まるでおどる
ようにはなびらが
ちってゆくわ・・・。
It is as if these ruffled
petals are dancing as
they melt away...

Girl: はかなさのなかにも
きらめくそのかがやき・・・。
Even within transience,
their radiance glistening...

Boy: 詩じんだなぁ・・・。
What a poet...

式

CEREMONY / STYLE

シキ

ex. 計算式* (けいさんしき) - math function
ex. 結婚式* (けっこんしき) - wedding
ex. 卒業式* (そつぎょうしき) - graduation

みてみて！テレビでけっこん式のばんぐみやってるよ。
きれいだねー。
？
？？
そんなことよりこのけいさん式がわからないよー！
式は式でもおおちがいね…。
わからなーい

First girl: みてみて！テレビでけっこん式のばんぐみやってるよ。
Hey, look! They're doing a TV show about weddings.

きれいだねー。
How pretty.

Second girl: そんなことよりこのけいさん式がわからないよー！ So what! I don't understand this math formula!

First girl: 式は式でもおおちがいね・・・。
Both words may use "shiki" but there's a big difference in meaning...

Second girl: わからなーい I don't get it!

CHAPTER

ショウ

ex. 楽章 (がくしょう) - musical movement
ex. 文章 (ぶんしょう) - sentence
ex. 腕章* (わんしょう) - armband

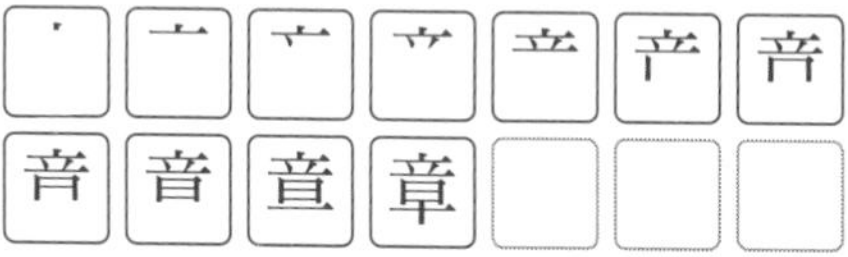

章

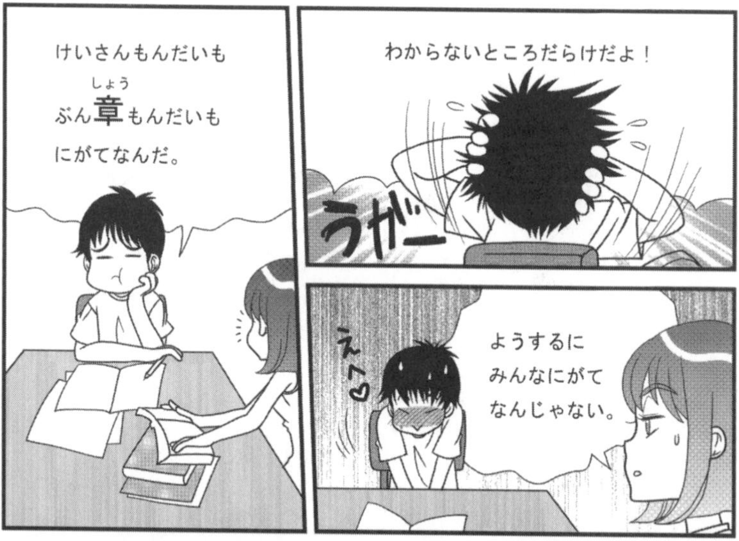

けいさんもんだいも
ぶん章(しょう)もんだいも
にがてなんだ。
わからないところだらけだよ！
うがー
えへ
ようするに
みんなにがて
なんじゃない。

Boy: けいさんもんだいもぶん章もんだいもにがてなんだ。
I'm bad at arithmetic and I'm bad at word problems.

Boy: わからないところだらけだよ！
This is full of stuff I don't get!
うがー (frustrated)

Girl: ようするにみんなにがてなんじゃない。
In other words, you're bad at everything.
えへ (embarrassed laugh)

SHINING

ショウ

ex. 昭和* (しょうわ) - Showa political era
ex. 昭和元禄* (しょうわげんろく) - mid-Showa
ex. 昭和史* (しょうわし) - history of Showa era

にほんのげんごうって
へいせいのまえは
<ruby>昭<rt>しょう</rt></ruby>わだったんだ。

そうだね。

こくみんのへいわを
ねがういみで
つけられたんだよ。

なんだかおもしろく
なってきたわ。

よかった。

Girl: にほんのげんごうってへいせい
のまえは昭わだったんだ。
So, in Japanese history, the Showa
period preceded the Heisei period.

Boy: そうだね。 Right.

Boy: こくみんのへいわをねがういみで
つけられたんだよ。
The government wanted a name that
represented peace for its citizens.

Girl: なんだかおもしろくなってきたわ。
That's really interesting.

Boy: よかった。 I'm glad you think so.

STATE / PROVINCE

す、シュウ

ex. 九州 (きゅうしゅう) - Kyushu
ex. 本州 (ほんしゅう) - Honshu
ex. 中州 (なかす) - sandbar

州

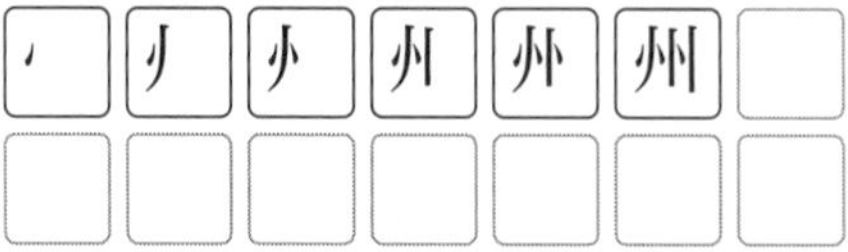

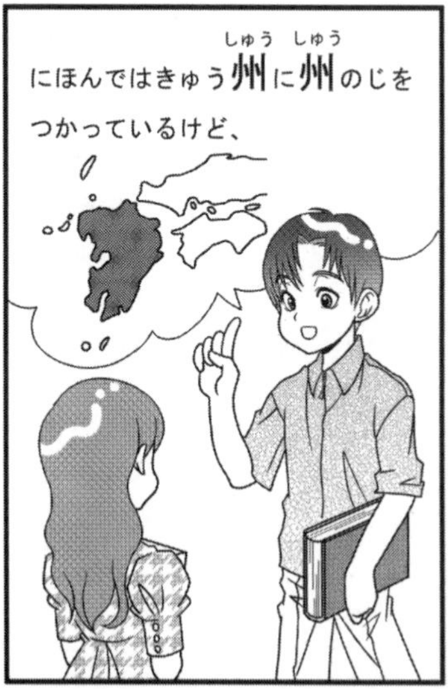
にほんではきゅう州に州のじを
つかっているけど、

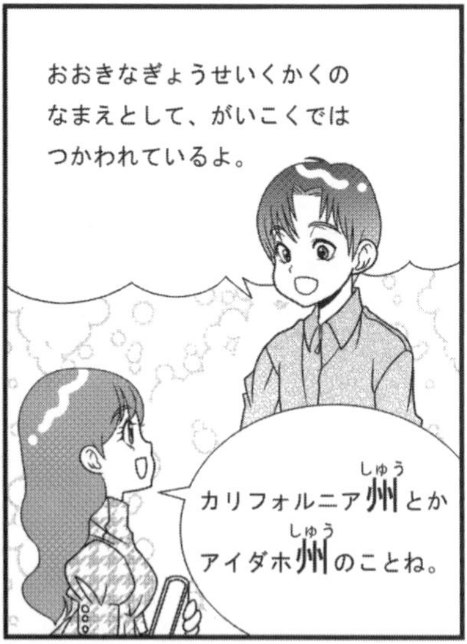
おおきなぎょうせいくかくの
なまえとして、がいこくでは
つかわれているよ。
カリフォルニア州とか
アイダホ州のことね。

Male student: にほんでは
きゅう州に州のじを
つかっているけど、
In Japan, the island of
Kyushu uses the shuu
character...

Male student: おおきなぎょうせいくかくの
なまえとして、がいこくではつかわれて
いるよ。 But shuu is also used for the
names of large districts in other countries.

Female student: カリフォルニア州とか
アイダホ州のことね。
Like California and Idaho.

PROCEED

進

すす(む)、すす(める)、シン

ex. 進行 (しんこう) - advance

ex. 進む (すすむ) - to make progress

ex. 前進 (ぜんしん) - progress

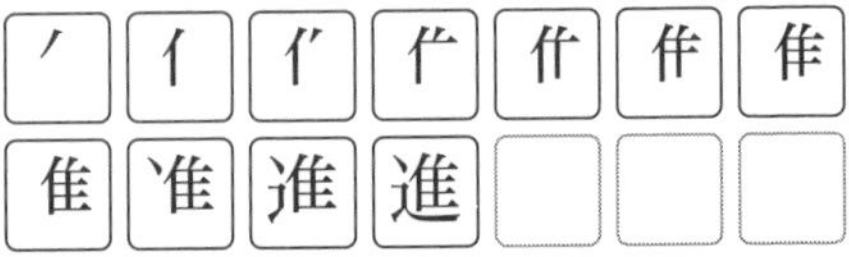

ねぇ…このままどうくつを進むの？
む？
ぼうけんかたるものぜん進あるのみ！
しゅっぱつ進こう！いくぞー！
バサ
バサ
バサ
わぁぁぁ!!

Boy on right: ねぇ・・・このままどうくつを進むの？
Umm... are we going to keep going into the cave like this?

Boy on left: む？ Huh?

Boy on left: ぼうけんかたるものぜん進あるのみ！
This is the only way we can advance the plot of our adventurous tale.
しゅっぱつ進こう！ いくぞー！
Let's move forward!! Go, go, go!
バサバサバサ (rustling of bat wings)

Both boys: わぁぁぁ！！ Yikes!!

CHARCOAL / COAL

すみ、タン

ex. 炭 (すみ) - charcoal

ex. 木炭 (もくたん) - charcoal (from wood)

ex. 炭酸飲料* (たんさんいんりょう) - soda

炭

バーベキューでつかう
もく炭もってきたよ。
ありがとう。
ドサ…
くすくす
くす
ぷっ
ど…
どうしたの？
炭でかおが
まっくろだよ。
!

First boy: バーベキューでつかうもく炭もってきたよ。
I brought the charcoal for the barbecue.

Second boy: ありがとう。Thanks.

ドサ・・・ (carrying something)

Second boy: ど・・・どうしたの？
What are you laughing at?

くすくすくすぷっ (giggling)

*People in crowd :*炭でかおがまっくろだよ。
Your face is black from the charcoal!

FAST

すみ(やか)、はや(い)、ソク

ex. 時速 (じそく) - speed per hour
ex. 速報* (そくほう) - quick announcement
ex. 速い (はやい) - fast

一	厂	冂	吂	申	束	束
束	速	速				

わぁ！

すごく**速**かったね。

そうだね。
じ**速**なんキロくらい
でていたのかな？

プワーン (roar of car's engine)

Both boys: わぁ！
Woah!

First boy: すごく速かったね。
That was fast.

Second boy: そうだね。じ速なんキロくらい
でていたのかな？
Yeah, how many kilometers per hour do
you think that was?

THOUGHT

ソ、ソウ

ex. 回想 (かいそう) - reflection; reminiscence
ex. 感想文* (かんそうぶん) - essay of thoughts
ex. 想像* (そうぞう) - guess

一	十	オ	木	村	相	相
相	相	相	想	想	想	

きょうは、なつやすみの
いろいろなおもいでを
かん**想**ぶんにしてもらいます。

は一い

えーと…。

……!!
……!?

いったいなにをかい**想**
しているのだろう…。

ふるふるふる

Teacher: きょうは、なつやすみのいろいろなおもいでをかん想ぶんにしてもらいます。
Today I'd like you to write an essay describing what you remember about summer vacation.

Students (in unison): はーい OK!

Both boys: えーと・・・。 Hmm...

ふるふるふる (shivering in fear)

Second boy: いったいなにをかい想しているのだろう・・・。
I wonder what he's thinking about...

OTHER

タ

ex. 他動詞* (たどうし) - transitive verb
ex. 他人 (たにん) - other person
ex. 他 (ほか) - other

ノ	イ	仂	他	他			

他のものにきを
とられるとあぶないよ！

キョロ

だいじょうぶ
だって！！

キョロ

他にんのふり、
他にんのふり。

First boy: 他のものにきを
とられるとあぶないよ！
It's dangerous to be distracted
by so many things.
Second boy: だいじょうぶ
だって！！It's fine!!
キョロキョロ (looking around)

バシャッ (splash)
どろ〜
(covered in mud)
あっ (gasp)

Second boy: 他にんのふり、
他にんのふり。
I don't know you, I don't
know you.

まってよー！！(wait up!!)

スタスタスタ (dashing)

COMPARE

タイ、ツイ

ex. 対 (たい) - versus
ex. 対抗* (たいこう) - opposition
ex. 対策* (たいさく) - countermeasure

対

こんどのあかぐみ対しろぐみの対こうじあいはぜったいにかつぞー！
赤組 白組
おぉー
せんせーい、なにか対さくはあるんですか？
あぁ、
対さくはまったく…
かんがえていないよ。
どわっ

Teacher: こんどのあかぐみ対しろぐみの対こうじあいはぜったいにかつぞー！ This time when the red team battles the white team, we will definitely win!

Students (in unison): おぉー Yeah!

Student: せんせーい、なにか対さくはあるんですか？ Sir, have you thought of any counter-strategies?

Teacher: あぁ、対さくはまったく・・・かんがえていないよ。 Oh, I've completely... neglected to think of any.

どわっ (students falling over in disbelief)

ORDINAL NUMBER

ダイ

ex. 次第に (しだいに) - gradually
ex. 第一 (だいいち) - the first
ex. 第六感* (だいろっかん) - sixth sense

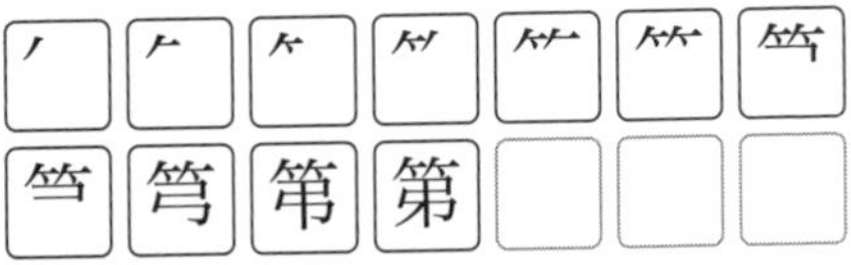

ノ	ト	ト	トー	トケ	トヶ	竺
笁	笃	第	第			

どうしたの？
うかないかおして。

じつは
つぎのじゅぎょうの
せんせいが
にがてでさ…。

だい
第いちいんしょう
からわるかったから…。

ガミガミガミ

だい
し第ににがてじゃ
なくなるって。
だいじょうぶよ。

そうだと
いいけど…。

Girl: どうしたの？
うかないかおして。
What's wrong? You look upset.

Boy: じつはつぎのじゅうぎょう
のせんせいがにがてでさ・・・。
Well, I've hit it off pretty bad
with the teacher of the next class.

Boy: 第いちいんしょうからわるかったから・・・。
I made a bad first impression...

ガミガミガミ・・・ (scolding)

Girl: し第ににがてじゃなくなるって。
だいじょうぶよ。Don't worry, it'll get better.

Boy: そうだといいけど・・・。If only that
were true... ポン (pat of the hand)

RESCUE / ASSIST

たす(かる)、たす(ける)、ジョ

ex. 助言 (じょげん) - advice
ex. 助手 (じょしゅ) - assistant
ex. 助ける (たすける) - to help

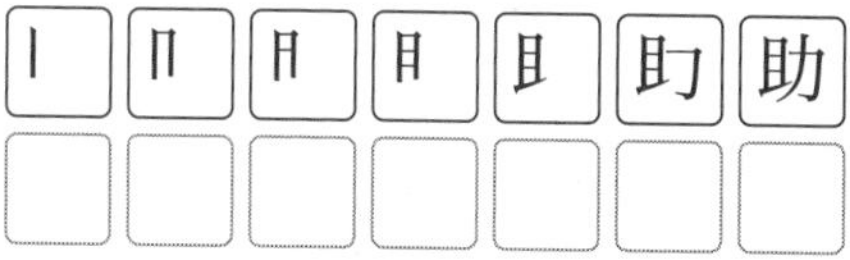

丨	冂	月	月	且	助	助

こまったわー。

イヤリングを
かたほうおとして
みつからないわ…。

<ruby>助<rt>たす</rt></ruby>けしましょう。

<ruby>助<rt>じょ</rt></ruby>しゅです。

えっへん。

おねがい
するわね。

たんていごっこ
なのかしら。

Mother: こまったわー。
Oh no...
イヤリングを
かたほうおとして
みつからないわ・・・。
I've lost
my earring!

Older brother: お助けしましょう。
こっちは、助しゅです。 Allow us
to help. Here's my assistant.
Younger brother: えっへん。
Ahem.
Mother: おねがいするわね。
Please help.

Mother: たんてい
ごっこなのかしら。
I wonder if
they're just playing
make-believe.

BALL

たま、キュウ

ex. 球根 (きゅうこん) - plant bulb

ex. 球 (たま) - ball

ex. 野球 (やきゅう) - baseball

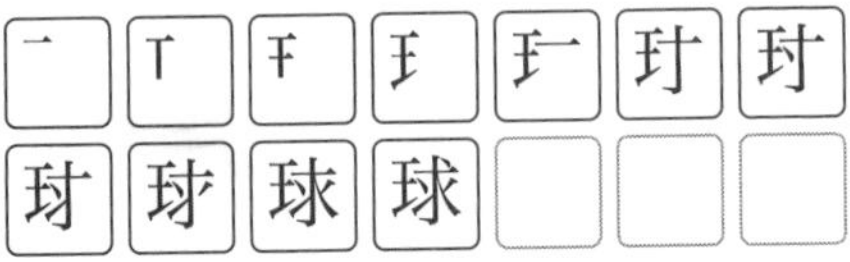

一	T	F	王	玌	珂	玗
玕	玗	球	球			

このあいだ、バッティングセンターで
じそく１５０キロの球をうてたよ！

すごーい！！

や球のボールってちいさいのに
うてるなんてすごいね。

えっへん！

First boy: このあいだ、バッティング
センターでじそく１５０キロの
球をうてたよ！
Just now at the batting cages I hit balls
pitched 150 kilometers per hour!!

Second boy: すごーい！！
That's awesome!!

Second boy: や球のボールって
ちいさいのにうてるなんてすごいね。
It's amazing you can hit a baseball
when it's such a small target.

First boy: えっへん！
Mmm-hmm!

DISCUSS

ダン

ex. 怪談* (かいだん) - ghost story
ex. 冗談* (じょうだん) - joke
ex. 面談* (めんだん) - interview

一	ニ	三	言	言	言	言	言

| 訳 | 訳 | 談 | 談 | 談 | 談 | 談 | |

そう**談**があるんだけど…。

げっそり…

いったい
どうしたんだ!?

じつはうちゅうじんに
きにいられてしまって
こまって
いるんだ。

たすけてくれよー！

じょう**談**じゃ
ねーよ!!

First boy: そう談が
あるんだけど・・・。
I need to talk about something...

げっそり・・・ (sunken cheeks)

Second boy: いったいどう
したんだ！？
What in the world happened!?

First boy: じつはうちゅうじんにきに
いられてしまってこまっているんだ。
Well, I've unfortunately attracted the
attention of a space alien.

たすけてくれよー！ Help me out here!

Second boy: じょう談じゃねーよ！！
This isn't funny!! あわあわ (panicking)

血

BLOOD

ち、ケツ

ex. 血液型* (けつえきがた) - blood type

ex. 献血* (けんけつ) - blood drive

ex. 血 (ち) - blood

ゆけつようの血がたりません！
けん血にごきょうりょくを
よろしくおねがいします！
けん血かぁ…。
たまにはしてみようかな。

Boy: ゆけつようの血がたりません！けん血にごきょうりょくを
よろしくおねがいします！
We still don't have enough donor blood! We'd really appreciate your assistance in our blood drive!

Girl: けん血かぁ・・・。たまにはしてみようかな。
A blood drive... I should try to donate sometime.

NEXT

つぎ、つ(ぐ)、シ、ジ

ex. 次元 (じげん) - dimension

ex. 次 (つぎ) - next

ex. 目次 (もくじ) - table of contents

次

このしごと たのむね。
あと これも。
はい。
次(つぎ)から次(つぎ)へと しごとがふえて いくよ～…。
ずーん
次(じ)かいの かいぎのしんこうは だれだっけ？
ぼくです！
またふえた…。

First man: このしごとたのむね。 Please take care of this.
Second man: はい。Sure.
Third man: あとこれも。This too.
Second man: 次から次へとしごとがふえていくよ～・・・。The jobs keep piling up one after the other.
ずーん (stressed out)
Woman: 次かいのかいぎのしんこうはだれだっけ？ Who's conducting the next meeting?
Second man: ぼくです！またふえた・・・。Me! Yet another job...

PLACE

ところ、どころ、ショ

ex. 所在地* (しょざいち) - address
ex. 長所 (ちょうしょ) - strong point
ex. 所 (ところ) - place

KOBAN

すみません、かどの**所**で
とけいを
ひろったので
とどけに
きたのですが。

おとしぬしがわかったら
れんらくするから、

はーい。

このようしに
きみのじゅう**所**や
れんらくさきをかいてね。

Woman: すみません、かどの所で
とけいをひろったのでとどけに
きたのですが。
Excuse me. I found a watch on the
streetcorner so I'm bringing it in.

(A koban is a small police station.)

Police officer: おとしぬしがわかったら
れんらくするから、このようしにきみの
じゅう所やれんらくさきをかいてね。
We'll contact you if we find the owner,
so please write your address and contact
info on this form.

Woman: はーい。 All right.

ORGANIZE

ととの(う)、ととの(える)、セイ

ex. 整頓* (せいとん) - tidy up
ex. 整理 (せいり) - sorting
ex. 整える (ととのえる) - to be prepared

ピシッ

へやの **整**り **整**とんは
かんぺき。

しょくじのよういも
整ったし、

あとはともだちが
くるのをまつのみ。

あっ…
きたみたい。

ピシッ (satisfied)
Woman: へやの整り
整とんはかんぺき。
Everything in this room
is completely tidy and in
order.

しょくじのよういも
整ったし、
All the food has been
carefully arranged...

あとはともだちがくるのを
まつのみ。Now all I have
to do now is wait for my
friends to arrive.
ピンポーン (doorbell)
あっ…きたみたい。
Ah! They must be here.

取

TAKE

とり、と(る)、シュ

ex. 取材* (しゅざい) - collecting data

ex. 摂取* (せっしゅ) - absorption

ex. 取る (とる) - to take

一	丅	F	F	耳	耳	耳ヲ
取						

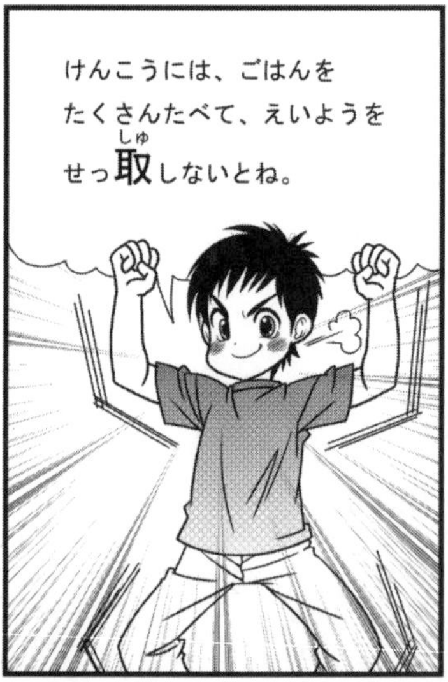
けんこうには、ごはんを
たくさんたべて、えいようを
せっ取しないとね。

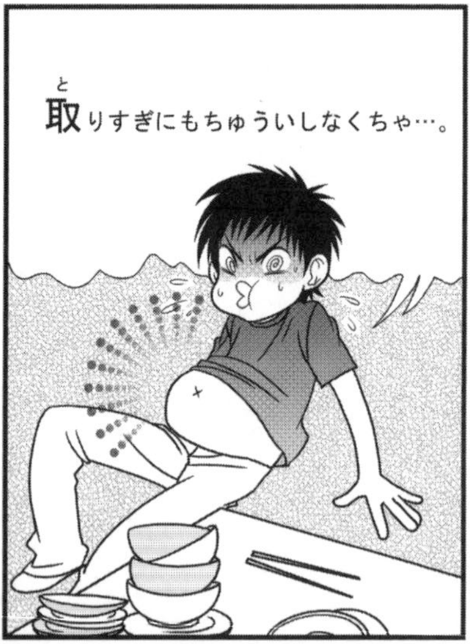
取りすぎにもちゅういしなくちゃ…。

Boy: けんこうには、ごはんをたくさんたべて、えいようをせっ取しないとね。
To stay healthy, I eat a lot of rice so I can absorb plenty of nutrients.

取りすぎにもちゅういしなくちゃ・・・。
But I have to be careful not to absorb too much...

BAGGAGE

荷

に、カ

ex. 集荷 (しゅうか) - pick up cargo
ex. 荷造り* (にづくり) - packing
ex. 荷物 (にもつ) - luggage

一	十	艹	芢	芢	荇	荷
荷	荷	荷				

かがり〜、
りょこうのじゅんびは
おわった？
カチャ
に
荷づくりがおわらないよー!!
ごちゃ
ごちゃ
に
荷もつが
おおすぎるのよ!!

Big sister: かがり〜、りょこうのじゅんびはおわった？
Kagari*, are you done packing for our trip?

カチャ (door opening)

Little sister: 荷づくりがおわらないよー!!
I'm not done packing!!

ごちゃごちゃ (things all over the place)

Big sister: 荷もつがおおすぎるのよ!!
That's too much luggage!!

*Kagari (かがり) is the younger sister's name.

ROOT

ね、コン

ex. 根性* (こんじょう) - willpower
ex. 大根 (だいこん) - daikon (japanese radish)
ex. 根元 (ねもと) - root

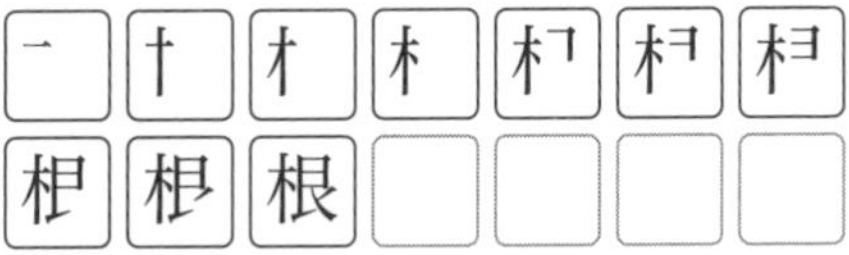

| 一 | 十 | 才 | 木 | 木 | 木 | 木 |
| 杞 | 柤 | 根 | | | | |

くさを**根**もとからとりのぞく
さぎょうってたいへんだね…。
かだんづくりもたいへんだぁ…。

もう！
根じょうないなぁ！！

もう…
だめ〜…。

でろーーん

Husband: くさを根もとからとりのぞく
さぎょうってたいへんだね・・・。
Pulling weeds up from their roots
sure is exhausting work...

かだんづくりもたいへんだぁ・・・。
Making a flower bed is just too hard...

Wife: もう！根じょうないなぁ！！
Come on!! You have absolutely
no willpower!

Husband: もう・・・だめ〜・・・。
Can't... go on...

でろーん (splayed out)

RIDE

の(せる)、の(る)、ジョウ

ex. 乗馬 (じょうば) - horseback riding
ex. 乗用車 (じょうようしゃ) - automobile
ex. 乗る (のる) - to ride

はやく、うんてんめんきょを
とって、じぶんのくるまに
乗りたいなぁ。

でも、乗るなら
乗ようしゃより
だんぜん
トラックがいいわ！

あんがい
おとこっぽい
のね…。

First girl: はやく、うんてんめんきょを
とって、じぶんのくるまに乗りたい
なぁ。
I really wanna get my driver's
license soon so I can drive my
own car.

Second girl: でも、乗るなら乗ようしゃより
だんぜんトラックがいいわ！ If you're
getting your own vehicle, it's gotta be a
truck! They're way better than sedans.
First girl: あんがいおとこっぽいのね・・・。
What an unexpectedly manly thing to say...
ブロロロロロ (vroooom) ぐっ (fist clench)

BRIDGE

はし、キョウ

ex. 石橋 (いしばし) - stone bridge
ex. 吊り橋* (つりばし) - suspension bridge
ex. 歩道橋 (ほうどうきょう) - pedestrian bridge

……。

あれ？
ほどう橋わたらないの？
はやくいこうよ。

ぼくは、いし橋を
たたいてわたるたち
だからしんちょう
なんだよ。

こわいよ～。

ただたんに
こうしょきょうふ
しょうなのね。

Boy: (speechless)
ヨロ・・・ヨロ・・・ (weak shuffle)

Girl: あれ？ほどう橋わたら
ないの？はやくいこうよ。
What's the matter, can't you
walk across a bridge? Let's go
already.

Boy: ぼくは、いし橋をたたいてわたるたちだから
しんちょうなんだよ。 I, uh, one must be prudent
and knock on a stone bridge before crossing it.
こわいよ～。 I'm scared!

Girl: ただたんにこうしょきょうふしょうなのね。
I think you are just afraid of heights.
ガタガタガタ (bones rattling) ぷっ (soft laugh)

CHANGE

ば(かす)、ば(ける)、カ、ケ

ex. 化学 (かがく) - chemistry
ex. 化ける (ばける) - to appear in disguise
ex. 変化* (へんか) - transformation

ノ　イ　イ　化

よのなかには
化がくではせつめいできない
できごともたくさんあります。

たとえば…。

じつは、わたしがタヌキの化けた
きょうじゅ
だったり！

ドロンッ

---

*Professor:*よのなかには化がくでは
せつめいできないできごとも
たくさんあります。
There are some things that
happen in the middle of the night
that even science cannot explain.

たとえば・・・。For instance...
じつは、わたしがタヌキの
化けたきゅうじゅだったり！
I'm actually a tanuki* disguised as
your professor!

ドロンッ (sudden transformation)

*A tanuki is a Japanese animal sometimes referred to as a raccoon dog.

拾

GATHER

ひろ(う)、シュウ、ジュウ

ex. 拾う (ひろう) - to gather
ex. 収拾* (しゅうしゅう) - coping
ex. 栗拾い* (くりひろい) - gathering chestnuts

きょうのくり拾いで拾ったせいかです！
ばっ
すごいりょうを拾ったねー。
どっさり
すげー。

First girl: きょうのくり拾いで拾ったせいかです！
Here are the results of today's chestnut-gathering expedition!

ばっ (revealed suddenly)

Second girl: すごいりょうを拾ったねー。
Wow, you really gathered a lot!

どっさり (a mountain of things)

Boy: すげー。
Amazing.

SECOND

ビョウ

ex. 秒 (びょう) - second
ex. 秒針* (びょうしん) - second hand (clock)
ex. 秒速 (びょうそく) - speed per second

ノ	二	千	禾	禾	利	利
秒	秒					

びょう
1秒もタイムが
ちぢんでるよ！
ベストタイムだね。

やったー！

Coach: 1秒もタイムがちぢんでるよ！
ベストタイムだね。
You cut your time by one second!
It's a new personal best.

Runner: やったー！
All right!

DEEP

ふか(い)、ふか(まる)、シン

ex. 深呼吸* (しんこきゅう) - deep breath
ex. 水深 (すいしん) - water depth
ex. 深い (ふかい) - deep

このいけ、ちいさいけど
深<ruby>深<rt>ふか</rt></ruby>いのかなぁ？

ちゃぽ　ちゃぷん

えーと…。

いけはちいさいが
すい<ruby>深<rt>しん</rt></ruby>3メートルいじょうある
…らしいよ。

しまった！

じゃぽん

Boy: このいけ、ちいさいけど
深いのかなぁ？ This lake, it's small
but I wonder if it's deep or not...
ちゃぽ　ちゃぷん (wading noises)
Girl: えーと・・・。 Umm...

Girl (reading guidebook): いけはちいさい
がすい深3メートルいじょうある・・・ら
しいよ。 It says here the lake is small,
however it's depth is over 3 meters.
Boy: しまった！ Oh, no!
じゃぽん (splash)

BRUSH

ふで、ヒツ

ex. 鉛筆* (えんぴつ) - pencil
ex. 筆順* (ひつじゅん) - stroke order
ex. 筆ペン (ふでペン) - brush pen

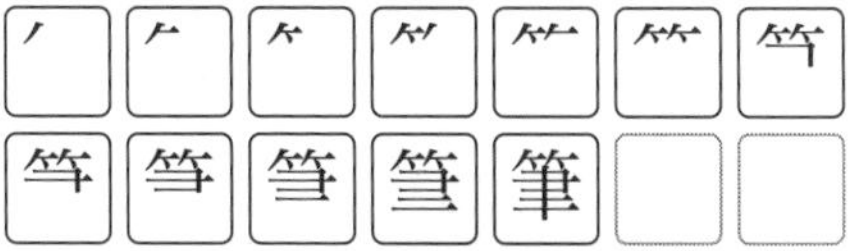

ノ	⺮	⺮	⺮	⺮	⺮	竺
竺	筆	筆	筆	筆		

みなさん
きょうはしゅうじを
します。

筆のよういは
できましたか？

筆じゅんに
きをつけながら

のびのび
かいてみましょう。

Teacher: みなさんきょうは
しゅうじをします。OK, everyone,
today we'll practice writing kanji.

Chalkboard: 習字 (penmanship)

筆のよういはできましたか？
Does everyone have their brushes
ready?

筆じゅんにきをつけながらのびのび
かいてみましょう。
Try to write with relaxed strokes while
paying attention to your stroke order.

Students (in unison): はーい Ye-esss!

Sign: 春 (spring)

MUSIC / CURVE

ま(がる)、ま(げる)、キョク

ex. 曲 (きょく) - song
ex. 曲線 (きょくせん) - curve
ex. 曲がる (まがる) - to turn

丨	冂	冄	曲	曲	曲

すてきな**曲**…
どこからきこえて
くるのかしら。

このかどを
曲がったあたりから
きこえてくるわ。

ストリートライブ
だったんだ。

Woman: すてきな曲・・・
どこからきこえてくるのかしら。
What a nice song... I wonder where it's coming from.

このかどを曲がったあたりから
きこえてくるわ。
I began hearing it right when I turned this corner.

ストリートライブだったんだ。
Oh, it's a street performance.

WHOLE

全

まった(く)、ゼン

ex. 全然* (ぜんぜん) - entirely
ex. 全部* (ぜんぶ) - all
ex. 全く* (まったく) - completely

ノ	八	亼	仐	仝	全	

きょうじゅうに、このかだい全ぶおわらせるなんてむりだよー！
全ぜんおわらないよー!!
うわーん
全くきみのいけんにどういするよ。
でも、サボっていたきみのせいだよ。

Boy: きょうじゅうに、このかだい全ぶおわらせるなんてむりだよー！
I can't believe they want us to finish this whole subject before the end of the day! It's impossible!

全ぜんおわらないよー！！
I'll never finish it all!!

うわーん (waahh)

Big brother: 全くきみのいけんにどういするよ。
I completely agree with you.

でも、サボっていたきみのせいだよ。
But it's your own fault for being a goof-off.

祭

RITUAL / CELEBRATE

まつり、まつ(る)、サイ

ex. 祭日 (さいじつ) - holiday
ex. 文化祭 (ぶんかさい) - cultural festival
ex. 祭 (まつり) - street fair

お祭ってにぎやかでいいよね。
でみせもたくさんあるしたのしいよな。
みて！あっちのおみせもたのしそうだよ！
わーい！
いくらお祭だからって…かいすぎだよ。
いってもむだか…。

First boy: お祭りってにぎやかでいいよね。Festivals are better when there's a large crowd.

Second boy: でみせもたくさんあるしたのしいよな。It's fun when there's a lot of booths, too.

First boy: みて！あっちのおみせもたのしそうだよ！ Look! That booth looks fun too!

わーい！ Yay!

Second boy: いくらお祭りだからって・・・かいすぎだよ。You always buy stuff like crazy at festivals. いってもむだか・・・。My words are falling on deaf ears...

PROTECT

まも(る)、まも(り)、シュ、ス

ex. 守る (まもる) - to protect
ex. お守り (おまもり) - good-luck charm
ex. 厳守* (げんしゅ) - strict observance

ヽ　ヽ　宀　宀　守　守

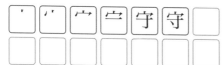

こうえんにはひとがたくさん
いるから、ルールを守って
あそぶようにね。

はーい。

1じかんごにもどること。
じかんげん守よ。

もぉ、

わかって
るって。

守らなかったなんて
ことがない
ようにね！

……。

Mother: こうえんにはひとが
たくさんいるから、ルールを
守ってあそぶようにね。There
are a lot of people in this park,
so obey the rules while you play.
Children (in unison): はーい。OK!

Mother: 1じかんごにもどること。じかんげん
守よ。Keep a strict watch on the time.
Girl: もぉ、OK. Boy: わかってるって。OK, OK...
Mother: 守らなかったなんてことが
ないようにね！You make it sound as if
you've never broken the rules!
Children: (speechless)

REALITY / TRUTH

み、みの(る)、ジツ

ex. 実験 (じっけん) - experiment
ex. 実際* (じっさい) - reality
ex. 実がなる (みがなる) - to bear fruit

実

このきって おいしそうな **実**がなるよね。

そうだね。

実さいは おいしくないけど…。

まずいっ！

づっ…

Girl: このきっておいしそうな実がなるよね。
This tree looks like it bears delicious fruit.

Boy: そうだね。
It sure does.

Girl: 実さいはおいしくないけど・・・。
In reality, though, it's not so good.

Boy: まずいっ！。
Yuck!

ぶっ (spitting out food)

SHORT

みじか(い)、タン

ex. 短気 (たんき) - short temper
ex. 短所 (たんしょ) - weak point
ex. 短い (みじかい) - short

| ノ | ト | 二 | 牛 | 矢 | 矢 | 知 |
| 矢口 | 矢口 | 矩 | 短 | 短 | | |

ちょうしょと
短しょ？

そうだな…
ちょうしょはがんばる
ところかな。

聞かないの。

かしてごらん。

短しょは…。

……。

ぐぐっ

短しょはきが
短いところね…。

なんだこのふた
かたいぞ。

あかない！

Boy: ちょうしょうと短しょ？そうだな・・・
ちょうしょはがんばるところかな。
My strengths and weaknesses? Well,
my strong point is probably persistence.

Boy: かしてごらん。Let me see...

Girl: 聞かないの。I didn't ask for help.

Boy: 短しょは・・・。My weakness is...
ぐぐっ (straining to open jar)

Girl: 短しょはきが短いところね・・・。
Your weakness is your short temper!

Boy: なんだこのふたかたいぞ。あかない！
The lid is stuck. I can't open it!

LAKE

みずうみ、コ

ex. 湖畔 (こはん) - lakefront
ex. 淡水湖 (たんすいこ) - freshwater lake
ex. 湖 (みずうみ) - lake

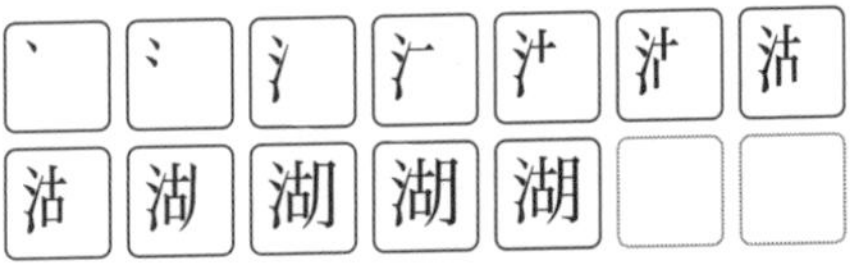

こんどのしゅうまつは
この湖しゅうへんにいかない？
しゅくはくしせつも
あるし。

湖はんのやどかぁ…。

おもしろそうね
いいわよ。

じゃぁ、
さっそくけいかく
たてなくちゃ。

First girl: こんどのしゅうまつは
この湖しゅうへんにいかない？
しゅくはくしせつもあるし。
Do you want to go out
to the lake this weekend?
They have lodging and
everything.

Second girl: 湖はんのやどかぁ･･･。
おもしろそうねいいわよ。
The lakefront? Sure, that sounds fun!
First girl: じゃぁ、さっそくけいかくたて
なくちゃ。All right, we have to start
planning now!
ばっ (opening a book quickly)

HARBOR

みなと、コウ

ex. 開港 (かいこう) - open port
ex. 漁港* (ぎょこう) - fishing harbor
ex. 港 (みなと) - harbor; port

`	`	`	氵	汁	洪	洪
洪	洪	洪	港	港		

みなと
港にたくさん
かざりつけがしてあるけど
なにかあるのかしら？

それはね。

こう
かい港150
しゅうねんのきねん
イベントが
あるからだよ。

Girl: 港にたくさんかざりつけがしてあるけどなにかあるのかしら？
There are a lot of decorations up at the harbor; I wonder what's going on?

Boy: それはね。Actually...

Boy: かい港150しゅうねんのきねんイベントがあるからだよ。
They're having an event to commemorate the 150th anniversary of the opening of this dock.

宮

SHRINE / PALACE

みや、キュウ、ク、グウ

ex. 宮廷* (きゅうてい) - Imperial Palace
ex. 宮殿* (きゅうでん) - palace
ex. 宮 (みや) - shrine

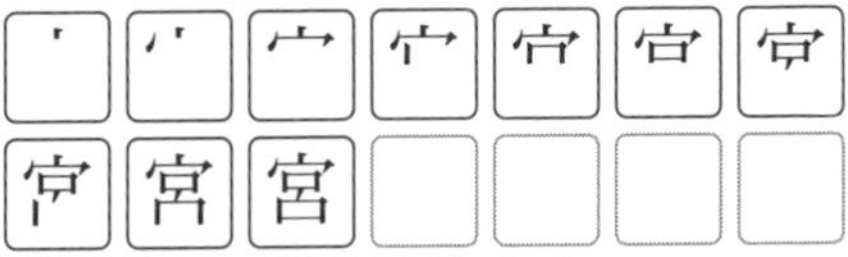

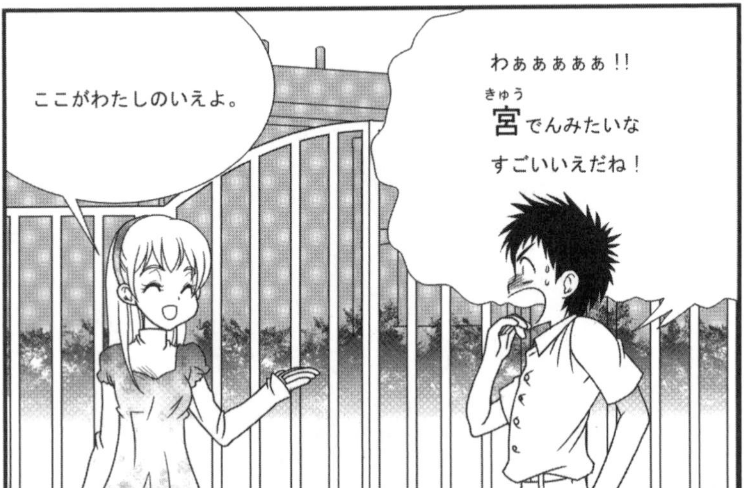
ここがわたしのいえよ。
わぁぁぁぁぁ!!
きゅう
宮でんみたいな
すごいいえだね!

*Girl:*ここがわたしのいえよ。
This is my house.

*Boy:*わぁぁぁぁぁ!!
宮でんみたいなすごいいえだね!
Whoaaa!! It's spectacular. It looks like a palace!

ONCE UPON A TIME

むかし、シャク、セキ

ex. 昔話 (むかしばなし) - folk tale
ex. 昔風 (むかしふう) - old-fashioned
ex. 昔々* (むかしむかし) - once upon a time

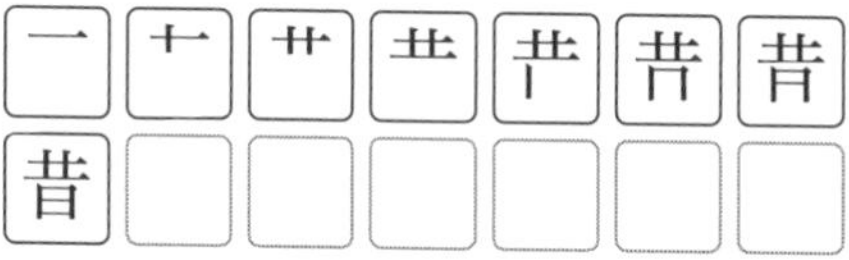

一	十	廿	昔	芇	昔	昔
昔						

むかしむかし
昔々、
もりのおくに

くまがすんでいました。

Mother: 昔々*、もりのおくに
Once upon a time, deep in the forest...

くまがすんでいました。
...there lived a bear.

*々 is a special character that indicates the
repetition of the kanji written before it.

FACING

む(ける)、む(く)、コウ

ex. 向上 (こうじょう) - improvement
ex. 方向 (ほうこう) - direction
ex. 向く (むく) - to face

向

´ 一 亇 向 向 向

じゃんけん

ぽん！

ほい。

あっち
むいて…

なんでまいかい
ゆびとおなじ
ほう向に向いちゃう
のだろう…。

Girl: じゃんけん
Rock, paper...
ぽん！
...scissors!
あっちむいて・・・
Hey, look over there!*

Girl: ほい。Made you look!
Boy: なんでまいかいゆびとおなじほう向に
向いちゃうのだろう・・・。
Why do I always turn and look in the
direction she points?

*In Japanese rock-paper-scissors, the winner points in
a direction and if the loser follows it's a double loss

REPORT

もう(し)、もう(す)、シン

ex. 申請* (しんせい) - application
ex. 申し込む* (もうしこむ) - to apply
ex. 申す (もうす) - to be called

丨	冂	冃	曰	申		

これから
申^{もう}しこみようしに
かきこむところよ。

たいかいの**申**^{しん}せいは
もうおわった？

Basketball player: たいかいの
申せいはもうおわった？
Did you finish signing us up
for the big game?

Coach: これから申しこみようしに
かきこむところよ。
I'm about to start filling in the
application now.

宿

LODGING

やど、やど(る)、シュク

ex. 宿泊* (しゅくはく) - lodging
ex. 新宿 (しんじゅく) - Shinjuku
ex. 宿 (やど) - manor

こんどのがっ宿じょのこときいた!?
?
??

『ゆうれいのでる宿』でゆうめいな宿はくしせつらしいよ。
えぇー!?
やだー!

Girl: こんどのがっ宿じょのこときいた!?
Have you guys heard about the boarding house we're staying at next?

Girl: 『ゆうれいのでる宿』でゆうめいな宿はくしせつらしいよ。
I heard we're spending the night at this place called "Ghastly Manor."

Others: ええー!? やだー!
Whaat!? No way!

SIDE

よこ、オウ

ex. 横断歩道* (おうだんほどう) - crosswalk
ex. 横 (よこ) - side; width
ex. 横綱* (よこづな) - highest rank in sumo

すみません。
としょかんへはどうに
いったらいいですか？

あぁ、
それなら。

じどうはんばいきの
横の横だんほどうを
わたってまっすぐいくと
ありますよ。

ありがとうございます。
たすかりました。

Boy: すみません。としょかん
へはどうにいったらいい
ですか？ Excuse me, what's
the best way to get to the
library from here?
Girl: あぁ、それなら。
Ah, if you want to go there...

Girl: じどうはんばいきの横の横だんほどうを
わたってまっすぐいくとありますよ。
Cross at the crosswalk alongside that
vending machine and it'll be straight ahead.
Boy: ありがとうございます。たすかりました。
Thanks, you've been a big help.

TAKE THE TEST!

The Japanese Language Proficiency Test has been held annually throughout the world since 1984. Administered by the Japanese government and the nonprofit Japan Foundation, the test evaluates and certifies the proficiency of non-native speakers of Japanese. There are four levels to the examination: Level 4 for beginners, Level 3 for intermediate students, Level 2 for those who are functionally literate in Japanese, and Level 1 for experts.

This book features 80 of the kanji students will need to know to pass Level 3 of the JLPT. Subsequent volumes in Manga University's *Kanji de Manga* series will help students prepare for the higher levels.

For more information about the Japanese Language Proficiency Test, including examination locations in your country, please visit the Japan Foundation's "JLPT Communications Square" website at http://momo.jpf.go.jp/jlpt/e/about_e.html.

Kanji de Manga

習字

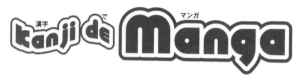

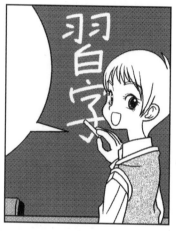

PRACTICE SECTION

KANJI INDEX

The 80 kanji featured in this volume of Kanji de Manga are indexed here based on their on-yomi and kun-yomi readings. This makes it easy to look up any kanji for which you know a pronunciation but cannot remember how the character is written. Because most kanji have more than one reading, you will find those characters listed multiple times in this index.

139 ページ

ALSO AVAILABLE FROM

MANGA UNIVERSITY

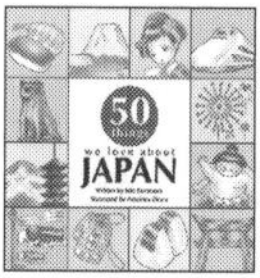
50
JAPAN

50 THINGS WE LOVE ABOUT JAPAN

By Edo Kurosawa & Atsuhisa Okura
ISBN-10: 4-921205-08-46 ISBN-13: 978-4-921205-08-9
Hardcover. English. 112 color pages. 5 inches x 5 inches.
US $9.99, CAN $11.99, UK £6.50

From *anime* to *karaoke* to *kaiten-zushi,* Nihon is number one when it comes to things that are cool. This fun little book features cute manga illustrations and delightful prose to offer the rest of the world a glimpse at what the Japanese love most about the country they call home.

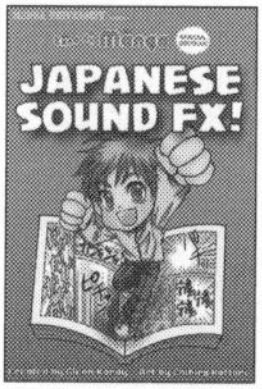
JAPANESE
SOUND FX!

KANA DE MANGA SPECIAL EDITION
Japanese Sound FX!

By Glenn Kardy & Chihiro Hattori
ISBN 4-921205-12-4
Paperback. English. 112 b/w pages. 5 inches x 7 inches.
US $9.99, CAN $11.99, UK £6.50

Onomatopoeia fill the pages of authentic manga. Written in hiragana and katakana, they are just as important to the story as the dialogue and drawings. This special edition of *Kana de Manga* uses all-new artwork to show Japanese onomatopoiea in action—and explain what they mean.

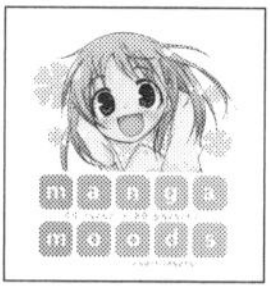
manga
moods

MANGA MOODS
40 Faces + 80 Phrases

By Saori Takarai
ISBN-10: 4-921205-13-2 ISBN-13: 978-4-921205-13-3
Hardcover. English. 96 color pages. 5 inches x 5 inches.
US $9.99, CAN $11.99, UK £6.50

Do you have mood swings? Well, you're not alone! The kawaii (that's Japanese for "cute") characters in *Manga Moods* know exactly how you feel! Whether they're giddy or grumpy, or something in between, these cuties always manage to put on their best faces. And while they're at it, they'll teach you how to speak a little Japanese, too.

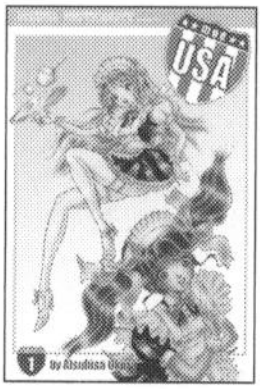
USA

MOE USA
Volume 1: Maid in Japan

By Atsuhisa Okura
ISBN-10: 4-921205-19-1 ISBN-13: 978-4-921205-19-5
Paperback. English. 160 b/w pages. 5 inches x 7 inches.
US $9.99, CAN $11.99, UK £6.50

Moe USA chronicles the antics of two all-American girls who land jobs as waitresses in a Tokyo maid cafe. Despite their "moe" (pronounced "moh-ay," Japanese slang for "super-cute") appeal, the girls seem destined for failure. That is, until they discover a couple of magical maid costumes that change their lives forever!

GLENN KARDY is the editor of several volumes in the renowned *How to Draw Manga* series of art-instruction guides, including *Getting Started*, the first book of its kind to be used at major universities in both the United States (UCLA) and Japan (Waseda). Glenn lives in the Tokyo suburb of Kawaguchi City with his wife, their daughter and a collection of Oakland A's bobblehead dolls.

CHIHIRO HATTORI, niece of legendary manga artist Eiichi Fukui, was a graphics designer at Tokyo-based TechnoArt before turning her attention full-time to her manga career. Chihiro and her husband live in Yokohama, where they enjoy fine food, fast cars and high fashion.

Cover illustrations by Chihiro Hattori
Art coordinator: Mari Oyama
Translator: Dale Rubin
Editorial assistant: Jakub Makalowski